BRITISH RA
IN THE 1970s AND '80s

Greg Morse

SHIRE PUBLICATIONS

First published in Great Britain in 2013 by Shire Publications, part of Bloomsbury Publishing Plc.

PO Box 883, Oxford, OX1 9PL, UK

1385 Broadway, 5th Floor, New York, NY 10018, USA

Email: shire@shirebooks.co.uk   www.shirebooks.co.uk

A CIP catalogue record for this book is available from the British Library.

Shire Library no. 753   ISBN-13: 978 0 74781 251 7

Greg Morse has asserted his right under the Copyright, Designs and Patents Act, 1988, to be identified as the author of this book.

Designed by Myriam Bell Design, UK.
Typeset in Perpetua and Gill Sans.
Printed in China through World Print Ltd.

17 18 19 20 21   11 10 9 8 7 6 5 4 3 2

COVER IMAGE
Sporting its original 'Inter-City 125' livery, HST No. 253 038 is seen at Taunton in 1982, beneath traditional semaphore signalling.

TITLE PAGE IMAGE
The interior of an 'Inter-City 125' First Class saloon, c. 1976. These trains brought high-speed travel to Britain and were a worthy flagship in BR's 'Age of the Train'.

CONTENTS PAGE IMAGE
'Deltic' 55019 *Royal Highland Fusilier* powers an express past the Scottish border on 15 July 1978. The train is mainly made up of 'Mark IId' carriages, whose introduction in 1971 allowed BR to provide its first non-supplementary fare air-conditioned services.

ACKNOWLEDGEMENTS
I am indebted to Julia Jenkins, Roger Badger, Dave Bennett (ASLEF), David Brown, Paul Chancellor (Colour-Rail), David Christie, Paul Clyndes (RMT), D.J. Fleming, Graham Floyd, John Foster, Irene Grabowska, John Heald, Derek Hotchkiss, Philip Hunt, Gerald Riley, Garry Stroud, Michael Woods, and STEAM Museum, Swindon. I would also like to thank Nick Wright and Russell Butcher at Shire Publications.

The illustrations are acknowledged as follows:

British Rail, pages 1, 14 (all), 15 (bottom), 17 (top), 34 (top), and 58; David Christie, pages 3, 4, 6–7, 17 (bottom), and 52; Colour-Rail.com collection, pages 10–11, 15 (top), 18, 19 (bottom), 20, 21, 24–5, 29, 31, 38, 39, 40 (bottom) and 57; L. F. Folkard/Colour-Rail.com, page 26; John E. Henderson/Colour-Rail.com, pages 9 (bottom) and 56; Science and Society Picture Library, pages 12 and 22; STEAM Picture Library, pages 34 (bottom), and 54 (top); Garry Stroud, cover and pages 9 (top), 19 (top), 27, 30, 32, 36, 43 (bottom), 44, 45 (all), 46 (bottom), 53 (bottom), and 59 (top); Topfoto, cover image; Michael Woods, page 8 (top). All other images are from the author's collection.

This book is dedicated to my late father, Pete Morse.

Shire Publications is supporting the Woodland Trust, the UK's leading woodland conservation charity, by funding the dedication of trees.

CONTENTS

INTRODUCTION

RAIN CLOUDS LOOM on a late afternoon; the air is sharp, the concrete platforms cold. A 'local' rasps in from the suburbs, filling the place with fumes, as a garbled message breaks from the tannoy. A ticket inspector shoves his hands in his pockets and stamps his feet to keep warm. In the distance, an express appears, its front end coated with brake dust and grime. The thrum of the diesel becomes the clunk of the coach wheels as they pass over pointwork and on to plain line. The driver eases the brake as the red signal nears, but before the train stops, doors fly open, and jumpers start running for connections ... appointments ... trysts.

Some make for Menzies, seeking *Custom Car* or *Look-in*; others wait for someone to help with cases and bags. Those with more time head to the buffet, or perhaps to the bar for a Watneys or gin. Few notice the lad studying the timetable, an all-line Rail Rover burning in his hand.

Doors slam, a whistle blows and a yellow tug rolls by to fetch trolleys of papers and parcels. One of the passengers sits on a bench, scribbling away with a pencil and pad. He makes a note here, he makes a note there – and then crosses it out and starts again. Later that evening, he'll open his act on a familiar tack:

British Rail sandwiches cost the earth – and taste like it!

'BR' – the butt of many such jokes – was formed in 1948, when the Great Western, London Midland & Scottish, London & North Eastern and Southern Railways were taken into public ownership, together with fifty smaller concerns. It was originally divided into six regions, controlled by the Railway Executive – one of five that answered to the British Transport Commission, which had been established to provide a 'properly integrated system of public inland transport and port facilities within Great Britain'.

The Railway Executive inherited over 20,000 locomotives, 56,000 coaches, a million wagons, 43,000 road vehicles, 650,000 members of staff and nearly 9,000 horses. Much of the rolling stock – and the track on which it ran –

Opposite: Though the railway changed rapidly in the 1970s and '80s, new and old continued to coexist in parts – as at St Pancras in 1982, where a 1950s enamel name board shares entrance duties with the double-arrow logo devised the decade after.

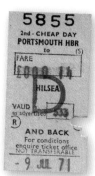

Above: Despite advances in technology, traditional card-board 'Edmondson' tickets would survive in pockets until 1989. This one dates from July 1971 and took its purchaser from Portsmouth Harbour to Hilsea and back for 14 new pence.

was in poor condition, having been heavily used and lightly maintained during the Second World War. Modernisation and renewal followed in the 1950s, which led to some service improvements, infrastructure upgrades and the replacement of steam by diesel and electric locomotives. The latter was achieved by 1968, and had been sped by Dr Richard Beeching, a director of ICI brought in by the government to make the railways pay. His tenure as Chairman, of both the Commission and (from 1 January 1963) the British Railways Board (BRB), was best known for the publication of the infamous

The east side of London Liverpool Street in May 1974. The station had remained much the same since the early 1960s, with the exception of the fashions, the yellow platform tugs, yellow bins and yellow ends on the trains.

Reshaping of British Railways report (1963), which led to the closure of numerous loss-making lines and stations, a greater focus on the block movement of freight, and the introduction of modern management techniques. These policies only contained BR's deficit, but Beeching's legacy also included better staff training and a sleek, corporate identity, featuring the famous 'double arrow' symbol and a new name: in January

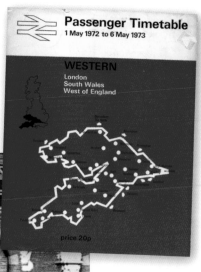

Passenger Timetable
1 May 1972 to 6 May 1973

WESTERN
London
South Wales
West of England

price 20p

Above: A Western Region timetable from 1972. BR originally comprised six Regions: the Eastern, London Midland, North Eastern, Scottish, Southern, and Western. The North Eastern was absorbed into the Eastern from 1 January 1967, but five would become six again with the creation of Anglia in 1988.

From 1 January 1976, BR dispensed with 'headcodes' to describe train types, replacing the four-character displays on the fronts of locomotives with two marker lights, as seen here on 50021 at Bristol Temple Meads in 1977.

A grimy Class 31 with a commuter train at Farringdon, London, in 1974. The coaches are non-corridor, and date from the early 1950s. Electrification in the late 1970s would see their replacement by 'open-plan' electric multiple units.

The National Traction Plan of 1968 spelled the end for many of the less successful diesel designs ordered in the 1950s. By 1979, however, some of the rest were nearing the end of their lives, while others would be subject to recession-led cutbacks. Here, at Swindon on 25 October 1980, a variety of locomotives await their fate.

1965, British Railways became British Rail, and would remain so for just over thirty years.

After several reorganisations – and chairmen – BR reached the end of the 1960s considerably leaner than when it began. In twenty years, locomotive numbers had fallen to just over 4,500, workshops had been halved to fourteen, and staff numbers had dropped to 296,000. But though route mileage had been cut from 20,000 to less than 11,000, the 1968 Transport Act pointed to a more stable future, setting down principles that would protect the loss-making lines that had social value and put the railway on a proper public service footing. To further this aim, it wiped out BR's

At Carlisle, 86239 stands with the Glasgow–Brighton 'Sussex Scot' in August 1988. Though blue is still the colour here, the Class 47-hauled train to the left carries 'large logo' livery, which had started to appear in the late 1970s. Many other liveries would follow in the 1980s.

9

debts and established Passenger Transport Executives (PTEs) in and around some of Britain's major urban centres to aid the provision of local bus and rail services. It also allowed BR's workshops division to manufacture for other industries. As a result, British Rail Engineering Limited (BREL) started trading in May 1970, with a turnover of around £100 million and a staff of 37,000.

Yet where investment was concerned, it was a case of *plus ça change*, BR still needing government approval for major projects such as signalling or rolling stock renewal. Sometimes it was allowed to spend its own funds; sometimes it was allowed to borrow – as with much of the £1,200 million spent on modernisation in the mid-1950s. Always it had to justify itself by making economies, selling assets or seeking new revenue streams; and always the papers would point out that it was all public money anyway.

For British Rail, the 1970s and '80s would be a time of contrasts and contradictions: when bad jokes about sandwiches and services veiled real achievements, like 'parkway' stations and high-speed travel; when television told of an 'Age of the Train', but Monday morning misery remained as commuter stock aged and grew ever more uncomfortable; and when new

electrification schemes were overshadowed by the Advanced Passenger Train, whose ignominious end came under the full media glare.

This book sketches a world of Travellers-Fare, Travel Centres and peak-capped Railmen – a difficult period, in which the rhyming optimism of old British Transport Film commentaries was supplanted by White Papers, balance sheets and acronyms, in which remnants of the old steam railway were modernised out of existence, and which began with the aftershock of Beeching, but ended with BR becoming the first nationalised passenger network in the world to make a profit.

A cyclist waits as a diesel multiple unit passes Saxmundham level crossing in June 1988. Not all crossings had full barriers like this one, some being left 'open'. A fatal collision at Lockington in 1986 would lead to the fitment of automatic half barriers to ninety-two open crossings by 1991.

See a friend this weekend

Inter-City makes the going easy
(and the coming back)

there are many rail travel bargains-ask for details

British Rail *Inter-City*

THE QUEST FOR
PASSENGERS

BRITISH RAIL LEFT THE 1960s looking forward to 'a decade of progress such as railways have never seen'. No longer in the red, it welcomed 'a new era', in which steam was gone and the 'conflicts between social and commercial responsibility' were over. Hereafter, it was 'free to act as a thoroughly commercial, profit-centred enterprise'.

On the surface, there was much to be optimistic about: continuous welded rail was replacing jointed track for a smoother, quieter ride; safety was improving; the southern half of the West Coast Main Line was enjoying the benefits of recent electrification, and – what with all the automatic level crossings, air-braked wagons and hovercraft – the past seemed to be getting left further and further behind.

On the other hand, costs were rising and inflation was threatening; many main lines were still controlled by semaphore signals and many loose-coupled goods trains still clattered over old-fashioned jointed track much as they had for over a century. And while it was true that more people who chose to travel by public transport went Inter-City, 1970 was also right in the middle of the rise in private vehicle ownership: BR had been worried when the number of cars on British roads exceeded three million, but this figure had nearly quadrupled – a fact that saw the railway's share of the total passenger market fall to just 8 per cent.

Perhaps unsurprisingly, the Board began to seek income from other sources, such as its Shipping Division, catering and hotels. BR was also one of the six largest landowners in Britain and earned further revenue by developing some of its property, as at Birmingham New Street, where a shopping centre was built on a raft above the station. This side of the business was one in which the Chairman, Henry Johnson, took a keen personal interest – so much so that he went on to join a leading property company when he left BR in September 1971.

Johnson had been a career railwayman, starting his working life before nationalisation. His retirement saw the appointment of someone quite different: the charismatic Richard Marsh, who – at forty-three – was the youngest of all BR leaders.

Opposite: A poster for Inter-City, c.1970, featuring the famous Monica.

Track and signalling

Traction and rolling stock

Above left: Colour light signalling continued to replace mechanical equipment throughout the 1970s and '80s, and Automatic Warning System (AWS) coverage followed this trend, growing from almost 3,200 track miles in 1970 to 7,013 by 1989.

Above right: Two gentlemen discuss matters of great import in a first-class compartment. This image is taken from British Rail is travelling... 1970, a brochure published to herald a new decade and 'a new era' for the industry.

Marsh was also a politician, who had succeeded Barbara Castle as the Labour government's Minister of Transport in 1968. In Whitehall, he took the unpopular step of authorising the closure of the 'Waverley' route (Carlisle–Edinburgh via Hawick) – a line earmarked by Beeching, but with a vociferous anti-closure campaign behind it. In office, he promoted the export of BR technology, proved to be a good spokesman and came with an awareness of the problems that further cost increases could create.

Doubtless with an eye to Ted Heath's Conservative administration, Marsh told British Transport Films in 1972 that 'if you spend money, then people will use the railways'. He was talking about a new type of station that had just opened at Stoke Gifford: 'Bristol Parkway', built near the intersection of the M4 and M5 motorways, with parking spaces for six hundred cars. The idea was to give motorists the advantages of an Inter-City station without the hassle of city centre parking and congestion. It was an immediate success, local residents soon realising that it was much more relaxing to reach London or the north by driving to Parkway for a direct train rather than battling their way to the middle of Bristol to get one from Temple Meads. However, this – and initiatives like the introduction of air-conditioning to East Coast Main Line services – was not quite enough to win back passengers.

Market research had found that, with journey times of up to three hours, rail was highly competitive with air and had the added advantage of delivering travellers close to the shops and office blocks. Beyond three hours, and

people tended to let the plane take the strain. Electrification, though a solution, was expensive and while the £55 million project to raise the wires from Weaver Junction (near Crewe) to Glasgow would be approved by the government in February 1970, it was clear that if rail were truly to compete with air, a new train would be needed. In fact, BR closed the 1960s with two possibilities, although it was unclear at that stage which would appear first.

The story had begun in 1964, when the Railway Technical Centre (RTC) opened in Derby, the company having decided to concentrate its

Above: Class 86 E3125 at Euston in June 1970 – the flagship station on BR's flagship West Coast Main Line. Note the overhead wires, from which 25kV AC power is collected by the pantograph on top of the locomotive.

Left: Another image from *British Rail is travelling … 1970*, showing the Lancastrian Grill at Euston, with its elegant views of the concourse and departures board. At the time, Euston's bars and cafés were proving so popular that they had to be extended.

research activities in one place. One of the RTC's early projects involved the problem of 'hunting' – an alarming, lateral wheel oscillation that tended to affect rigid two-axle wagons running on rigid continuous welded rail. There had been several serious derailments where trucks had seemed to simply leap from the track, but as hunting was also evident when 'Mark I' carriages were run at high speeds, it was clearly a bar to reducing journey times too. A research programme was developed, headed by Alan Wickens, who had joined BR from the aerospace industry. His team – which included many other aerospace engineers – devised a new suspension system that could achieve a good quality ride at all speeds on any type of track. The knowledge gained from this work was applied to bogie vehicles in 1967, and materialised in the 'Mark III' coach, which was capable of 125-mph travel and which – at 75 feet – was some 8 feet longer than a conventional railway carriage. This meant more passengers in fewer vehicles and therefore lower maintenance costs.

It had been assumed that anything travelling faster than 125 mph would need a total rethink in terms of track alignment and signalling. The Japanese National Railway's famous 'bullet trains' were operating at speeds of up to 130 mph on purpose-built lines with gentle gradients and few curves. BR knew that to achieve the same in Britain would involve time-consuming Parliamentary Bills, public enquiries – and public money.

BR's Shipping and International Services Division was rebranded 'Sealink' in 1970. This postcard shows the 4,370-ton motor vessel *Vortigern*, launched in 1969 as the first of a new generation of multi-purpose ferries.

But the RTC wondered whether faster trains could be run on existing infrastructure by improving rolling stock suspension. From this idea, and its 'anti-hunting' work, the Advanced Passenger Train (APT) was developed, which could attain speeds of up to 155 mph, minimising passenger discomfort by tilting into curves – a feature which would be particularly beneficial on the West Coast Main Line, where it still took over six hours to reach Glasgow from Euston, owing to the tortuous nature of its steep, northern section.

The project secured partial government funding in 1968 and clearance to construct a four-car experimental train (APT-E), test track and laboratory

Above: Bristol Parkway c.1972. The 'Parkway' concept had been tested at New Pudsey in the late 1960s. Similar stations at Birmingham International (1976) and Southampton Airport Parkway (1986) would follow.

Left: In 1968, Brush Traction's experimental diesel-electric *Kestrel* was handed over to BR for testing. It had the requisite 4,000-hp engine for 125-mph running, but was too heavy to be driven faster than 100 mph. Withdrawn in 1971, it was later sold to the Soviet Union.

Opposite top: Delivered in 1959, the 'Blue Pullmans' featured air conditioning and sound insulation, but the development of the 'Mark II' carriage soon made the extra fare for such services seem expensive and irrelevant. The 'Pullmans' were withdrawn by May 1973; this example awaits its fate at Swindon that August.

the following year. Traction would be supplied by a gas turbine, which – like an electric motor – could deliver twice as much power as diesel, but – unlike an electric motor – would not confine test runs to electrified areas and limit the service potential of later production designs. As a result, the team entered into an arrangement with British Leyland, which was developing turbine technology for possible use in heavy goods vehicles.

Watching from the sidelines were the traditional railway engineers, a number of whom were not impressed with these young aerospace 'upstarts' and their lack of experience. Though newcomers can bring fresh new ideas, this 'old guard' had seen too many mistakes being made, tests being re-run and purchase orders being re-raised. They felt sure an alternative was possible, and by the end of 1968 had sketched out rough plans for a 'High Speed Diesel Train' (HSDT), which could reach 125 mph.

BR's new Chief Engineer of Traction and Rolling Stock, Terry Miller, could see the potential of the HSDT and – in light of growing concerns about the APT – submitted a formal proposal to the Board in early 1969. Henry Johnson was sufficiently impressed to give the HSDT his public approval, adding that if the APT did not prove itself within the next four to six years, BR would need something reliable to fall back on – not official authorisation, but very useful for helping to move the project forward. By the autumn of 1970, £800,000 had been granted for the development of a prototype, whose specification now included the new 'Mark III' carriage design.

The HSDT was complete within two years. Like the 'Blue Pullman' units, it featured a 'power car' at each end, as this was the only way of attaining

Right: The HSDT and APT were not the only prototype designs produced in the early 1970s. Seen at Waterloo in 1973 is no.4001, one of the experimental 'PEP' electric multiple units, which led to BR's 'second generation' fleet, comprising Classes 313, 314, 315, 507 and 508.

the requisite 4,500 hp, there being no suitable single, lightweight unit available at the time. However, the arrangement also brought tremendous operational advantages by removing the need to release locomotives and re-marshal trains at terminal stations.

With its sleek, clean lines and Cyclops-like front end, the HSDT certainly looked impressive as it sliced through the landscape. Yet through that single windscreen lay a problem, for the lack of cabside windows

The operational benefits of using locomotives at both ends of a train were demonstrated on the Scottish Region, which introduced accelerated services between Edinburgh and Glasgow using pairs of Class 27 diesel-electrics in May 1971. Here, no.5409 stands alongside a 'Deltic' at Edinburgh Waverley three years later.

Unveiled in July 1972, the gas turbine powered APT-E was the first tilting train to feature an active mechanism that could respond to the characteristics of each bend.

and proper provision for a secondman was challenged by the unions, who argued that two fully qualified drivers should be present in all trains that travelled above 100 mph. As the APT-E had also been designed with 'single-manning' in mind, and as there was uncertainty about whether the extra responsibility for high-speed driving would be recognised financially, they refused to allow their members to work on either train until a settlement had been reached.

The APT team welcomed the 'blacking' at first, as it let them rectify the many electrical faults that had been plaguing the turbine control units. However, by the time an agreement was reached and testing resumed in August 1973, almost a year had passed. Furthermore, the Organization of Arab Petroleum Exporting Countries had imposed an oil embargo in response to the USA's support of Israel during that year's Arab–Israeli war. This led to fuel shortages and widespread price rises, forcing British Leyland to cancel its automotive turbine programme and the Board to consider electric traction for the production APT (although Leyland did agree to continue its engineering support until 1976, in order to let BR complete the experimental phase of the project).

The union dispute with the HSDT had ended in December 1972, BR having fitted a proper secondman's seat and agreeing to double manning with extra pay when trials involved speeds above 100 mph. These began on the East Coast Main Line the following month, and soon saw the train live up to its name. By June 1973, it was breaking records: on the 6th, it matched the world diesel traction record of 133 mph set by Germany's 'Fliegender Hamburger' in 1939; on the 11th, it reached 141 near York on a run so smooth, the driver said he could have 'rolled a cigarette or written a letter'; on the 12th, it powered its way to an impressive 143.2 between Northallerton and Thirsk.

The East Coast Main Line would enjoy further high-speed runs in the years ahead, but the first production batch of HSTs was destined to transform Western Region services out of Paddington. With twenty-seven trains under construction, the prototype was transferred to Old Oak Common depot for staff training. It entered service on 5 May 1975, working existing 100-mph schedules. BR's catering division – by now re-branded Travellers-Fare – devised a special 'high-speed' menu, which included draught beer for the first time on a British mainline train. Not only did many passengers partake of a pint of Whitbread (32p) – or a cup of tea (8p), or fruit pie (16p) – many marvelled at the effortless speed, the comfortable seats, the spaciousness and the automatic vestibule doors. In fact, the train proved so popular that some altered their travel plans just to ride on it.

In comparison, the APT-E was little more than a laboratory on rails at this stage. Yet it was destined to attain even greater speeds once it too had migrated westward.

The HSDT passes Chippenham on 4 June 1975. The use of the current 'Pullman' livery was an attempt to make the train stand apart and create a heightened sense of quality. The production version would be more egalitarian.

Part of a priceless private collection

The Rugby Portland Cement Co. Ltd: 50 ton glw Bulk Cement Wagon. Designed for movement of powdered materials, equipped with air assisted discharge system. Builder: Charles Roberts of Wakefield.

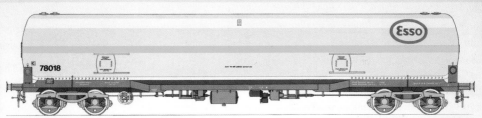

Esso Petroleum Co Ltd: 90 ton glw LPG Tank Car. For conveyance of liquefied petroleum gases – Propane and Butane – under pressure, in trainloads. Side valve discharge. Builder: Charles Roberts of Wakefield

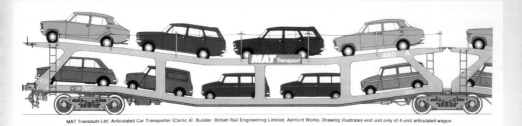

MAT Transauto Ltd: Articulated Car Transporter (Cartic 4). Builder: British Rail Engineering Limited, Ashford Works. Drawing illustrates end unit only of 4-unit articulated wagon

Just three exhibits from private collections of over 18,000 modern, high-capacity wagons that form part of industry's huge investment in Railfreight.

 **Railfreight**

The big name behind the biggest transport jobs

THE NETWORK
SPREADS

'Shall I pull it now, guvnor?'
'No, lad – after the next bridge, count to 35. Then do it.'

T HE LAD WAITS; the bridge passes; the count begins. The blue-grey train whistles fast along the straight. Inside, staff sort letters as they ride. Outside hang the mailbags, black against the sky. A lever is pulled, a net opens wide and they're scooped into the coach with a resounding CLUNK.

This is the Travelling Post Office (TPO) – the modern-day 'Night Mail' – still crossing the border, still bringing the cheques, postal orders, birthday cards and bills. The line-side exchange apparatus had been pioneered by the Grand Junction Railway in 1838. In 1911, there were 245 such installations on the British railway network; by 1967, there were just thirty-four.

The fact was that, like everything else, the postal business was changing. True, there was increasing mechanisation – as at Bristol's new concentration depot, with its conveyor belts and network of express parcels trains. But there was also increasing competition from air and a decreasing need for BR involvement.

The cutbacks had started in 1968, when the Post Office introduced a two-tier system of delivery and decided that there was no need for slower second-class mail to be carried by train. Demand for the more expensive first-class service fell away and with it went the need for so many TPOs. Withdrawals began in 1972, by which time the use of line-side apparatus had also ceased, the final pick-up coming at Penrith in October 1971. Henceforth the scene would be relived only in miniature, courtesy of Triang-Hornby and its successors (until the preservation movement amassed sufficient hardware for full-size demonstrations).

Penrith itself was destined to see many more changes: within a year, the stub of the Workington line – the 'Keswick branch', listed for closure by Beeching – had succumbed; within another two, West Coast Main Line

Opposite: A poster from c. 1974, advertising the increasing number of air-braked, privately owned wagons in use on BR. Customers would be actively encouraged to buy their own vehicles over the next fifteen to twenty years, as it cut BR's wagon maintenance liability considerably.

Class 25 no. 7571 arrives at Bradford Forster Square in May 1971 amid a plethora of parcels vans and trolleys. The Post Office did not seek long-term renewal of its parcels contract with BR after 1974, choosing a combination of road and rail in a bid to cut costs.

electrification had progressed from its existing limit at Weaver Junction, through the town and on towards Scotland.

Known to the industry as the 'Weaver to Wearer' project, this scheme involved the erection of over 15,000 steel masts and the suspension of some 1,650 miles of wire. Much of the route still used semaphore signals – not conducive to fast running – so these were replaced with multi-aspect colour lights, controlled from new signal boxes at Warrington, Preston, Carlisle and Motherwell, along with the existing installation at Glasgow Central (albeit extended). Some bridges also had to be raised to give sufficient clearance to the overhead equipment, while a combination of continuous welded rail and track realignment allowed speeds to be raised, and vital minutes to be shaved from the timetable.

BR had introduced a six-hour service between Euston and Glasgow in 1970 by using pairs of powerful diesels on the section north of Crewe, with its punishing gradients at Shap (1 in 75) and Beattock (1 in 67). When electric traction took over the whole route in May 1974, many were astonished at the ease with which the new 5,000-hp locomotives sailed up

Out with the new. Class 50s 406 and 449 take a Glasgow-bound service through the Lune Gorge in 1971, beneath a fairly empty M6. Electrification would see the locomotives moved to the Western Region within five years.

In with the old. BR had withdrawn main-line steam in 1968 and banned most preserved engines from January 1969. After much negotiation, this was lifted in 1971 and steam returned, first in the form of ex-GWR 'King' no. 6000 *King George V,* seen here pounding up Dauntsey Bank that October.

the inclines. Suddenly five hours was possible – not quite the four promised for the future by the APT, but good enough to see passenger numbers rise by 40 per cent over the coming year.

Growing at a comparable rate was the 'merry-go-round' (MGR) network, whose trains carried coal from colliery to power station, loading and unloading automatically at low speed. From the first test run in 1965, conversions had continued apace, such that by 1971 twelve power stations had been equipped with the loop lines, hoppers and discharge gear needed to facilitate this highly efficient mode of operation (so efficient in fact that a similar system was soon set up at Immingham Docks to speed the passage of imported iron ore to the British Steel plant at Scunthorpe).

'Block trains' like these had been advocated by Beeching, who saw a need to get away from wagonload traffic – with all its in-transit transhipment and re-marshalling – to the comparative simplicity of trainload operation. BR had already tested the waters with its 'Condor' and (later) 'Speedfreight' container services, but the 1960s saw the growth of the Freightliner concept, which used larger containers and longer trains. There were seventeen Freightliner terminals by 1968 and, though much of the initial traffic involved short-distance domestic hauls, the situation improved when it was realised that rail was ideal for carrying containers to and from ports. Tilbury was duly added to the Freightliner network in 1970, with Felixstowe and Southampton (Maritime) joining in 1972. By the end of the decade, some 42 per cent of the company's cartage would come from this source.

Class 47 47202 takes charge of a loaded MGR service in 1974. At the power station, the train will be emptied automatically while running at ½ mph – a system that greatly improved the efficiency of BR's coal operations.

Part of the block trains' success lay in their use of air brakes, which are technically superior to their vacuum-powered counterparts. This had been recognised back in the 1950s, but BR had baulked at the operational upheavals that conversion would bring. However, as time moved on, so did technology; research by the APT-E team led to the introduction of a prototype air-braked wagon that could be hauled at 75 mph. For managers, this offered a chance to compete in the 'sundries' market, which was being lost, thanks to the introduction of faster and heavier lorries, the growth of the motorway network, BR's rationalisation of its own goods facilities and its general neglect of that side of the business hitherto. Now, marketing was stepped up, co-operation between the various freight-handling functions was increased and an order for a production run of the new wagons was placed. Delivery began in 1969, with the first fully air-braked freight service following in October 1972. These overnight trains, which ran initially between Bristol and Glasgow, were essentially sets of mini block workings, coupled together for the common part of their journey. This reduced re-marshalling and increased the chance of a 'next day delivery' for customers.

While the 'air-braked network' (ABN) slowly spread, an innovative system of wagon and traffic management was also being developed. Both the Western and Eastern Regions had experimented with traffic control techniques, but America's Southern Pacific Railroad had since developed a Total Operations Processing System (TOPS), which used computers to monitor the position and use of rolling stock across an entire organisation. The Board had committed to £10 million of investment for TOPS in 1971; by 1975, it was fully operational and – together with the ABN – slowly started to turn the wagonload situation round.

With this, the APT-E reaching a record-breaking 152.3 mph on test, the first production High Speed Train (HST) power car erected, and the electrification of the West Coast Main Line complete, the casual observer might be forgiven for thinking that BR was on the ascendant. But though the 1968 Transport Act had brought financial stability, the subsidies provided to fund loss-making, socially valuable lines were falling every year. Furthermore, the contemptuous attitude to railways now evident in Whitehall was starting to be shared by the car-owning classes, for whom train travel was something their parents had done in the days of steam. Even enthusiasts were blaming management for the mess their beloved industry was in.

The hoppers being hauled by this Class 31 are 'unfitted', meaning that they have no continuous brake capacity, being equipped with handbrakes only. On trains like these, the guard will keep a hand on the brake handle in his van to make sure the couplings remain taught and don't snap. A few unfitted freights clanked on until 1983, traditional coal and scrap flows lingering longest.

All this irked Marsh, who bemoaned the 'well-known fact that the nation is divided between 27 million railway experts and 190,000 of us who earn our living on the railways'. More irksome, though, was the government, which he believed to be selling the railway short. 'In terms of capital investment for renewal, research, development and improvement,' he wrote in the Board's 1972 Annual Report, 'the railways' share has not been comparable with the millions poured into other forms of transport.' New motorways and trunk roads, he went on, 'represent a national investment every year more than five times greater than investment in British Rail, and even then most of the railway investment is to keep the system going.' With ministers asking questions about the viability – and size – of the network, Marsh pointed out that analysis showed there to be *no* viable network size and urged the government to accept that 'the social benefit to the community as a whole by keeping it intact was far greater than the book-keeping loss'. Yet he was fighting a losing battle, as rising inflation was turning any chance for investment into a call for cuts.

Edward Heath's attempts to beat inflation by capping wage increases had brought him into conflict with the unions. In particular, the National Union

Like BR's small-consignment collection and delivery service, Freightliner was transferred to the new National Freight Corporation from 1969. BR retained a 49 per cent stake, but regained the rest in 1978 in the hope of revitalising the brand. Here, 40012 takes a 'liner' through Bangor.

of Mineworkers (NUM) was pushing for a pay rise commensurate with the cost of living, launching an overtime ban that became a strike when negotiations failed. The Arab–Israeli war had driven up oil prices, making imports impossible, but now coal stocks were dwindling too. To reduce electricity consumption, Heath imposed a three-day working week from midnight on 31 December 1973. By the time it ended in March, Heath had been replaced by Harold Wilson and a new Labour government, which seemed to see Marsh's point, its Railways Act of 1974 reducing BR's capital debt from £438.7 million to £250 million and offering financial aid to businesses for setting up private sidings. The Act also replaced the individual payments for passenger services brought in by the 1968 Act with one Public Service Obligation (PSO) grant. This was a vital step forward in the financial relationship between the railway and the government, giving new security and self-respect to the management and helping to safeguard BR's regional passenger business.

For a while, at least…

Diesel and electric locomotives were reclassified in 1968 renumbering following from c.1973, as one-, two-, three- and four-digit numbers became five-digit ones. Class 87s like 87026, seen here at Carlisle in 1974, were the first to receive the five digits from new.

AGE OF THE TRAIN?

A SMALL BOY STANDS with his father at Swindon station, hoping to see one of the new '125s' before they head home. A shunter rumbles a rake of vans to the works while a '31' waits with a parcels train. All is quiet and it looks like they'll be disappointed, but then a blink of yellow catches the sunlight. The boy feels his fear-excitement rise as the whining, shining, double-ended beast speeds towards them. He jumps as the first power car screams past, and again as the rear one follows, fear turning to joy as the train zooms into the distance.

On board, a woman steadies her hand on the yellow panelling as she brings a tray of drinks back to her family. At the table opposite, a man puffs a pipe and doodles on his crossword, while a little girl tests the automatic vestibule doors once or twice too often. And who could blame her? They were so much nicer than the wooden ones in the older carriages. The toilets were cleaner too...

The first HST set – 253001 – had been transferred to the Western Region in April 1976 and was soon joined by others, allowing driver training to begin in earnest during the summer. Some sets entered passenger service that August, running to a maximum speed of 100 mph. From 4 October, however, all the design and development work, the track and signalling upgrades, the training and train planning came together with the launch of the 125-mph timetable and a world where Bristol was a mere seventy minutes from London; and where passengers could enjoy BR's 'Great British Breakfast', as their train terrified rabbits from their line-side resting place, sending them scampering in all directions. Henceforth, small boys who wrote to Jimmy Savile's BBC television programme, *Jim'll Fix It*, asking to drive a train would find themselves in the cab of an HST. Yet when they returned to the studio, it would not be Richard Marsh who regaled them with their commemorative badges, but a new man: Peter Parker.

Marsh had decided not to request that his statutory five-year appointment be extended, having become disillusioned with both Labour and Conservative governments, who failed to see that long-term planning and clearly defined

Opposite: BR was justly proud of the HST, which it saw as a 'worldbeater' and a 'shop window for Britain'. In time, the trains would also serve Leeds, Bradford, Aberdeen, Paignton, Plymouth and Penzance. Here, 253003 leaves Swindon for Bristol Temple Meads in January 1977.

Right: A young family enjoys the delights of second class, HST style. Note that the commodious table does not align with the window – a problem that would not have been suffered by passengers travelling 'first'.

Above: A badge produced by BR in the late 1970s to celebrate the excitement of travelling by HST (or 'Inter-City 125', as the trains were also known).

Right: Peter Parker (right), BR Chairman 1976–83, meets the management at BREL's Swindon Works. He was knighted in 1978.

objectives were essential for BR. He was also disappointed that the 1974 Act, while offering grants for businesses to set up rail facilities, made no mention of *socially necessary* freight services. By his own admission, however, his heart had been darkened by the death of his wife in a car crash the year before. It was a tragic end to an uneasy tenure, which saw steam return to the main line, the development of high-speed travel and the introduction of TOPS, but which also suffered strikes, three-day weeks, soaring oil prices, galloping inflation and falling passenger numbers as fares doubled to keep pace with costs.

Parker's appointment was announced in March 1976; he became a part-time Board member the following month and took over in the September. In fact – and unbeknown to press and public – he had been Barbara Castle's first choice after Stanley Raymond's departure in 1967. A great enthusiast and motivator, Parker was prepared to do battle on behalf of BR and wanted to shore up 'the crumbling edge of quality' that threatened parts of the system. As he also had a neat line in public relations, it can be no coincidence that television was soon extolling the virtues of a new 'Age of the Train', though it had to be said there was some truth in

The 1974 Railways Act offered grants to businesses wishing to set up rail facilities. Many linked with the air-braked network (ABN), which was rebranded 'Speedlink' in 1977. By 1982, there were eleven 'Speedlink' routes linking Britain's major ports and cities. Here, 33116 takes a service though Southampton.

Few would have foreseen the rise in popularity of steam's replacements. Yet as time passed, spotters found themselves following locomotives like the 'Westerns' – BR's last diesel-hydraulic class, finally withdrawn in February 1977. A month before the end, D1023 *Western Fusilier* waits at Swindon with an enthusiasts' special.

the marketing company's claim, passenger numbers rising wherever HSTs were deployed. Drivers seemed just as enthusiastic, many Western Region men being quick to join the unofficial '140 Club' (until speed governors were installed to cut off the power at 128 mph). A pity, then, that guards were less happy with the small compartment they were given at the rear of each power car (better accommodation would eventually be provided in a new design of coach).

HSTs took over some East Coast Main Line services in May 1978. The Eastern Region was disappointed not to receive a full roster at first, but found that many travellers were willing to wait for a '125' even if it meant standing for part of their journey. Those who took the 10:00 'Flying Scotsman' from May 1979 found the trip from London to Edinburgh had shrunk to just 4 hours 37 minutes – including a stop at Newcastle.

By now, the combination of increased speeds, more services (twenty-four a day between London and Bristol, against just fourteen in 1967) and improved ticket deals – like the 'AwayDay' (1976) and '17 Day Return' (1977) – were starting to reinvigorate express train travel. Indeed, Parker announced a surplus of £58.3 million in the Board's 1978 Annual Report, and pointed out that the financial objective agreed with the government had been improved upon for the third year running. Like Marsh, he could see the need for clear objectives, but decided BR would write its own, including an assumption that the levels of subsidy and investment would remain constant (adjusting for inflation), and that the size of the network would not change. The government agreed for a while, but would ultimately aim to reduce the cash demand.

In the meantime, HSTs were allowing commuters to live further away from their London offices. Soon, smart executives would settle into the same seat in the same coach day after day, waiting for that last journey of the week and its promise of a gin or scotch. Soon, semi-official social clubs would spring up among the regulars ... just as long as they lived in Reading, or Swindon, or Peterborough.

The trouble was that most commuters did not live on the high-speed routes, but on the suburban networks of the Eastern and Southern Regions. On the former, services from London's dingy Liverpool Street had not changed for over twenty years, ninety-four trains calling at Gidea Park, just as they had in 1955, 1965 and 1970; on the latter, the twenty-year-old BR 'Mark I' electric multiple units had recently been augmented by even

The HSTs' limited capacity for mail led the Post Office to consider alternative modes of transport. In response, BR provided extra, short-formation parcels trains. Its own parcels service – Red Star – continued to operate station to station, while vans like this one (seen at Weymouth Quay in 1977) would deliver door to door until 1981.

In 1974, the Labour government – mindful of a post-oil crisis need to reduce British dependency on the motor car – requested that BR reprieve certain lines that it already had permission to close. One such was the Inverness–Kyle of Lochalsh route, beloved by backpackers and enthusiasts. In this view, 26024 sits at Kyle with a short train in June 1978.

more – the Southern preferring the standardised approach where new builds were concerned. Each day, tens of thousands of Reginald Perrins agonised over their crosswords and their lives from crowded compartments, while their underlings clung to grab straps as they lurched over the pointwork into Cannon Street, London Bridge or Waterloo. But both pitied the poor souls on the Great Northern route into King's Cross, who endured compartment trains with no corridors, in which many an unwanted conversation was struck up as business men and women wound their way to work from Hatfield and Stevenage. Thankfully for this last group, electrification was on the way.

Sanctioned by the government in 1971, progress had been hampered to some extent by management insistence that no more than six minutes' delay be imposed on inter-city traffic. There was also much work to be done, including major alterations at King's Cross, a new flyover at Welwyn Garden City, new maintenance facilities at Hornsey and over fifty bridges, which had to be raised, renewed or reconstructed to make way for the overhead equipment. Nevertheless, full inner suburban services to Hertford and Welwyn Garden City began in November 1976, using the Class 313, BR's first 'second

generation' electric multiple unit (EMU), which featured smooth-riding bogies, rapid acceleration, and power-operated doors.

On the main line, electrification had been given a boost by the success of the Euston–Glasgow scheme, leading BR to consider it in the wider sense once again. The difference now was that the East Coast's place at the top of the list had been taken by the St Pancras–Sheffield route, the Board anticipating government approval of the self-contained commuter section between St Pancras and Bedford. This came in November 1976, but despite it, and more financial aid from the Passenger Transport Executives – Greater Glasgow, for example, buying sixteen 'second generation' EMUs for the re-opened 'Argyle line' – it remained clear that electrification had its limits. This meant that many suburban and rural services remained in the hands of diesel units that were well past their best. While some travellers still loved the forward-facing views that were possible – and which had been such a selling point when these trains were introduced in the 1950s – they rattled and shook, and were – to many – best avoided. Unfortunately, the prototype replacement (Class 210) – though a high-quality design capable of carrying over two hundred people at 90 mph – was over-engineered and proved too expensive to be a long-term solution. Many PTEs objected

The 1973 oil crisis opened government eyes to the need for more coal. This meant more trains – and more freight locomotives. Brush Traction won the contract for the 3,250-hp Class 56, but – lacking workshop capacity – subcontracted to Electroputere in Romania. The first '56' was delivered in 1976, but manufacturing faults led BR to bring the project 'in house'. Here, one of the original batch, 56016, passes Sheffield.

Although some pre-nationalisation units featured powered doors, the replacement programme for slam-door stock truly began from 1976 with the arrival of the 'second generation', derived from the 'PEP' design of 1972 (see page 18). This badge, produced to advertise Great Northern electrification, features the new Class 313.

The smart new way to London

and asked for a cheaper option. The result would see a return to the railbus concept of BR's early days, but first a refurbishment programme for the best of the old stock was begun, involving the fitment of replacement engines, modern upholstery, new floor coverings, new toilets and fluorescent lighting.

By this time, the Scottish Region had replaced its 'top and tail' services on the Edinburgh–Glasgow route with rakes of 'Mark III' coaches worked by Class 47s, which had been specially adapted to allow them to be driven from their own cabs or from a driving trailer at the remote end of the train. This retained the operational advantages of the earlier push-pull system, but the new motive power was capable of maintaining speeds of 100 mph, which – coupled with the comparative luxury of the 'HST' coaches – offered a step-change in service quality.

Elsewhere, as the ad campaign began, it seemed like the 'Age of the Train' was already passing: on the Western, passengers were being lost to the M4 and M5 motorways, while on the London Midland, the 'sparks effect' of West Coast Main Line electrification was waning in the face of fare increases and the launch of highly competitive Anglo-Scottish flights by British Airways.

Luckily, the Advanced Passenger Train was just tilting round the corner. . . .

A Class 40 and a '25' flank a 'driving brake second open' – or 'DBSO' – at Glasgow Queen Street in December 1979. The new push-pull service, brought in to replace ailing Class 27s, began earlier that year and was later extended to Aberdeen.

SERPELL, STRIKES
AND SECTORISATION

Five days before Christmas, and the pantograph is raised on the train of the future, its stylish livery and promise of power planned to coax long-distance passengers back from the air. Not that the APT is ready for passengers just yet, for this is a test run, on which pipes are puffed and instruments are checked as she tilts her way over the sinuous northern section of the West Coast Main Line.

> … passing Quintinshill, the driver 'notches up' and the speed climbs higher. Before Beattock, they've reached 162.2, breaking the record and setting another that would stand for twenty-three years …

Driver training began soon after, but hopes that a public service could be launched in October 1980 were dashed by a derailment, and problems with the tilt mechanism, gearboxes and brakes. By now, the project was being run from within the Chief Mechanical & Electrical Engineers' department, a re-allocation that had cost it many of the former aerospace engineers who conceived and shaped the experimental phase. Reorganisations and rigid procedures slowed progress further and caused management focus to slip. All the while, pressure to prove that the train could carry fare-paying passengers was mounting.

In the event, BR took a risk and decided to run a limited APT service from 7 December 1981. At first it looked like the gamble would pay off: the outward run was good, the train arriving at Euston just 4 hours and 13 minutes after leaving Glasgow (two minutes early!); but the return suffered from jammed doors, frozen brake pipes and another tilt mechanism failure. The papers talked of food flying across tables, drinks spilling into laps, and passengers suffering motion sickness (leading one wag to dub APT-P the 'queasy rider'). Soon, reporters pounced on the train's every woe, comparing it unfavourably to the HST, asking why it had taken so long to be developed and whether Britain really needed it anyway. All good questions, but the answers would only come after more

British Rail's Advanced Passenger Train

InterCityAPT

reorganisation and the introduction of a new style of management.

In January 1982, BR split its operational division into five Sectors: Inter-City, London & South East, Provincial, Railfreight, and Parcels. This would eventually disband the Regions and put BR on more of a business footing than even Beeching had envisaged. In time, each Sector would develop its own identity, but the main idea was to allow their directors to keep a close eye on running costs and overheads, with a view to cutting subsidy, creating confidence and building the case for investment. It sounded like the perfect solution to BR's problems, although some managers remembered – *knew* – that companies bled when reorganised, and feared that fragmentation would erode the clear chains of command and communication essential to safety.

Sectorisation had been hinted at after the 1979 General Election, which had seen Labour ousted by the Conservatives following a series of strikes over a public sector pay freeze imposed to control inflation. Parker and the Board realised that there would be little chance of Margaret Thatcher's new regime investing in rail unless something was done to increase productivity. With this in mind, they published *Challenge of the '80s* that November, which outlined their aim to develop the railway's commercial strengths, but also stressed the need to reform the operation and manning of trains, terminals and engineering establishments.

The railway had seen such change before, many good men leaving in the late 1960s, their artisan skills made worthless by the demise of steam. Some drivers who stayed lost their sense of self-worth, no longer heroes of the footplate. Firemen, who – as secondmen – did little but tend the soon-to-be-obsolete carriage steam heating equipment, now cost money BR didn't have; so too did guards, especially on the passenger side, where the introduction of more multiple units with powered doors meant that – in theory – more trains could be worked by the driver alone.

In fact, the difficult question of 'driver only operation' (DOO) had come up in 1975, when BR was awaiting delivery of the Class 313s. Back then, fears over union action dominated the Board's thinking and little progress was made. Now it was on the agenda again, but if productivity were to be increased with any effectiveness, flexible rostering would also be needed to cope with the ebb and flow of traffic and increase the amount of time drivers actually drove while on shift. The St Pancras–Bedford ('Bed-Pan') route may have been electrified in 1981, and 'second generation' units may have been waiting to work it, but the National Union of Railwaymen (NUR) – while agreeing to flexible rostering – would not agree to DOO. The Associated Society of Locomotive Engineers and Firemen (ASLEF), on the other hand, was happy enough with DOO (its members were drivers, not guards), but would not accept flexible rostering, wishing to maintain the eight-hour day agreed sixty-three years before. Both issues were also tied up with a pay claim, which BR tried to withhold to get leverage on the rostering question.

Several forty-eight-hour strikes, stoppages and overtime bans later, a tribunal ruled against the Board, although a deal struck at arbitration on

In 1979, BR started a club for young enthusiasts, offering travel discounts and other concessions. By the early 1980s, it had been renamed 'Rail Riders' and made much use of APT imagery, as this badge shows.

Opposite: A leaflet promoting the 'prototype' APT (APT-P), which broke the UK rail speed record by reaching 162.2 mph on 20 December 1979. In order to maintain such speeds with twelve carriages, APT-P required two power cars in the middle of the train, as positioning them fore and aft like the HST would have caused their pantographs to create a bounce in the contact wire.

The demise of the 'Deltics' came in January 1982. In this 1981 view, 55009 *Alycidon* waits at Peterborough with a special train for the Nene Valley Railway.

Though BR was working under a directive to maintain the system at its 1974 size, in July 1981 it closed the 'Woodhead' route between Manchester and Wath, which was expensive to maintain and worked with non-standard DC electric equipment. Here, Class 76s 028, 025 and 016 wait at Rotherwood stabling point shortly before the end.

productivity soon failed, forcing a return to the table. The situation worsened when the NUR – buoyed by the initial tribunal success and fearing a proposed run-down of BR's workshops – announced a strike of its members from 28 June 1982. BR used national advertising in a bid to halt the action, while Parker wrote directly to staff, warning that the strike jeopardised their pay increase and their jobs. He wrote again on the 23rd, warning that it was now 'one minute to midnight'; within 48 hours, the NUR strike collapsed, but almost immediately ASLEF re-entered the fray and announced an indefinite withdrawal of labour from 4 July over BR's decision to impose flexible rostering from the 5th. Its patience run out, the Board announced in the second week that it would close the railway down and sack the strikers. After pressure from the Trades Union Congress, a settlement was reached with ASLEF four days later.

The crisis was over, but the truth was that no one came out of it very well: drivers found themselves portrayed as backward-looking and unpatriotic, Parker's reputation for good labour relations was in tatters and ASLEF failed to block flexible rostering. Yet perhaps the most severely hit was the business

Left: BR saved more money by rationalising station facilities. At Exmouth, a grand Southern Railway structure was replaced by a smaller modern one in 1976. As at many other locations, a 'bus shelter' also appeared on the platform. The 15:20 for Exeter St David's does its best to ignore the downgrade on 30 September 1980.

Below: BR's prototype 'second generation' diesel-electric multiple unit – the Class 210, seen here at Didcot in 1983 – was a high-quality design, but ultimately too expensive for squadron service.

itself, the dispute costing BR at least £60 million. In a year that saw freight go into free-fall and passenger figures plummet, this was a loss it could have done well without. The Board tried to ease the situation by reducing fares and the number of services, but Whitehall's refusal to finance further HST sets meant that some of the planned routes were worked with a mixture of HSTs and traditional loco-hauled trains. There were also implications for the APT project, it now being obvious that twelve-car formations would never

Right: The solution to the diesel multiple unit problem was a return to the 'railbus' concept of the 1950s. A prototype was introduced in 1981, but the production classes soon followed. Sporting West Yorkshire PTE livery, this Class 141 is seen at Leeds in 1984.

Below: When main line steam ended in 1968, BR was left with the three narrow-gauge engines in use on the Vale of Rheidol line in Wales. This was sold off to the Brecon Mountain Railway in 1989. Here, no. 8 *Llywelyn* leaves Aberystwyth in September 1984.

be filled at current West Coast passenger levels. Add in the need to replace ageing rolling stock, renew miles of track and fit modern signalling, and it was clear that only a large cash injection would keep Parker's 'crumbling edge of quality' from crumbling away completely.

There were two strands to think about: the core business of running trains, and the subsidiaries like Sealink and Travellers-Fare. BR had reorganised the latter as separate functions and hoped to sell shares to raise funds

Railrover
Where you like, when you like.
from 1 March to 31 October 1981.

This is the age of the train ⇌

Red Star goes like there's no tomorrow.

Top left: BR's market research revealed Jimmy Savile to be the public's most-trusted celebrity for advertising purposes. Surprised by this, Parker asked the result to be checked. Its confirmation saw Savile go on to front BR's 'This is the Age of the Train' campaign from 1980. In 2012, Savile's posthumous reputation was destroyed after revelations of serial sexual abuse.

Top right: Leaflet for BR's Red Star express parcels service, c. 1983. Red Star started trading in 1963, and was carrying five million parcels a year by the end of 1979. Profitable in the 1980s, it became a separate division in 1988, though hopes for an increase in business via the Channel Tunnel were dashed by recession in the early 1990s.

and help them flourish. At first, the government seemed amenable to the suggestion, but had changed its mind by October 1981, believing a sell-off to be the most effective way of reducing BR's drain on the public purse. British Transport Hotels was the first to go, in 1983; the rest would follow within six years. Yet, as Marsh had found the decade before, Whitehall remained just as 'short-termist' where investment in the core was concerned, its approval for the electrification of the East Anglian main lines in December 1981, for example, being soon cut back by the rejection of two sections around Cambridge. A question mark also continued to hang over the East Coast Main Line.

The strike had not helped the cause, but Parker could see a glimmer of light in the form of an independent review that had come out of his discussions with the Department of Transport, and which was being led by BRB member Sir David Serpell, who had been part of the Stedeford Committee, a special advisory group set up by the government in 1960 to find ways of reducing the cost of modernisation (*inter alia*).

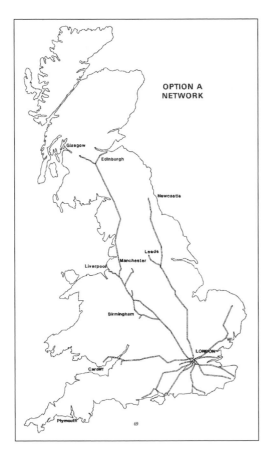

OPTION A
NETWORK

Glasgow

Edinburgh

Newcastle

Leeds
Manchester
Liverpool

Birmingham

LONDON

Cardiff

Plymouth

69

Serpell's infamous 'Option A'. In the 1970s, Marsh had worked out that even the smallest network would incur 'astronomical' costs in getting to that size (by pulling up track and so on). Serpell and his committee claimed not to have calculated the expense of drastically cutting route mileage.

Serpell, who left the Board to take on the role, was regarded by both sides as a safe pair of hands, but his committee's report – *Review of Railway Finances*, published in January 1983 – belied his reputation and seemed to lack focus. The document was critical of BR management, aspects of its ticketing policy and engineering costs, which could (it said) be pruned by getting rid of BREL. It also castigated the Board for being over-optimistic in its appraisal of 'high-risk' projects like the APT, and concluded that line closures would be needed if subsidies were to be 'lowered substantially'. To illustrate the point, the committee presented six network options, from a 'high-investment' version consisting of the existing 10,370 route miles (less a planned reduction of 300) to the 'Beeching-like' Option A, which assumed a network size of just 1,630.

Many of Serpell's findings were not revelations, having been freely admitted by the Board, whose members spoke with unguarded self-criticism in the hope that something supportive might emerge; instead, the report seemed to argue against investment, failed to consider service quality and did not acknowledge reforms that were already in hand, such as substantial staff reductions and the installation of automatic level crossings.

The Board had little choice but to shunt the whole thing into a siding, which it did by nudging the media towards Option A and the threat of commuter fare increases, and by publishing a formal response, which – while accepting that improvements could be made in engineering and government interaction – condemned the report as 'disappointing, inaccurate, implausible and misleading'. Richard Marsh, by now a life peer, also told the House of Lords that he found it 'extraordinary' that no evidence had been gathered from overseas railways. He went on:

> The curious and peculiar thing is that no passenger rail system anywhere in the world can break even. Countries as different as France, Germany,

Japan, Italy, Switzerland and Canada ... face similar problems, and yet the committee did not think to ask any of them what they had been doing over the past 20 or 30 years.

Shelved pending the June 1983 General Election, the Serpell Report quickly lost all credibility. Parker would later write that it had at least 'cleared the air'. In time, it would also give BR the impetus to pursue efficiency and 'firm up' its investment management practices. By then, though, the railway would have a new Chairman.

Parker had been invited to stay for another five years, but chose a three-year extension to work on the productivity question and steer the government towards a longer-term plan. He knew the next phase of BR's development had to be led from within and Robert Reid, who had joined the London & North Eastern Railway as an apprentice in 1947, was the ideal candidate. Parker – a popular man, who laid the foundations of Sector management and fought hard for investment in the APT and electrification – finally left BR in September 1983. For some, the railway was about to enter a new golden age.

Some, but not all.

Increases in bulk steel and oil traffic took Class 47s away from MGR workings and created the need for a new locomotive. BREL won the contract and the first Class 58 emerged from Doncaster Works in 1982, featuring an innovative modular design.

49

TOWARDS THE 1990s

I shall be looking for lower unit costs, better quality service and better value for money.

So SAID BOB REID, soon after becoming BR Chairman. It had taken time for the appointment to be made, partly because of a General Election in the summer and partly because the government had wanted another 'outsider', favouring the then head of Thorn EMI, Sir Richard Cave. But Cave wanted to be a part-time deputy and Parker wanted Reid. In some ways the two were very different: Parker, the great motivator, was happy to fight Whitehall on policy and funding; Reid, the brusque, task-oriented manager, was keen to get the job done within government guidelines. Yet both had seen sectorisation as the way forward.

Parker got his wish, Reid going on to preside at a time when BR began to flourish, as new liveries replaced the old, receipts started to rise and relics of the steam age vanished with gathering speed. And though the company's next marketing slogan – 'We're getting there' – would be a poor heir to 'This is the Age of the Train', it came to encapsulate that second half of the 1980s with some accuracy.

Unsurprisingly, Reid's contract required him to operate freight and parcels on a commercial basis, increase private sector participation and reduce the PSO grant by a quarter. It also required him to make no more major closures. Soon after he took over, however, BR announced its intention to shut the spectacular (but loss-making) Settle & Carlisle line. An unpopular move, this had been part of a deal with the Heath government to win support for electrification north of Crewe. Indeed, BR had closed all stations on the line bar Settle and Appleby West in 1970, diverting and reducing traffic such that, by 1981, the route was handling only a few trains a day. With the cost of maintaining the Ribblehead Viaduct climbing, closure notices went up in December 1983. Plans for a sell-off would follow four years later, but a public campaign, coupled with an astonishing increase in passenger numbers, saw the move blocked by the government. This left the Tunbridge Wells West–Eridge line with the dubious honour of

Opposite: Green-liveried Class 40 D200 takes a 'special' on from the Ribblehead Viaduct in April 1984. BR's closure plans for the Settle & Carlisle were cancelled by the government in 1989, thanks partly to a surge in traffic, which saw annual journeys rise from 93,000 in 1983 to 450,000 by the end of the decade.

47 701 *Saint Andrew* is seen at Edinburgh Waverley sporting the ScotRail livery first seen in 1984. The North British Hotel rises in the background; it had been sold the same year during the 'privatisation' of BR's British Transport Hotels subsidiary.

Opposite, top: A leaflet advertising Gatwick Express services for 1987. This was two years after the re-allocation from Network SouthEast to InterCity, which also saw the original slogan and neat variation on the standard BR logo 'change hands'.

Opposite, bottom: A resplendent NSE electric multiple unit prepares to leave Eastbourne. Note the lamp-posts, whose red colour scheme was somewhat easier to apply than the rolling stock livery.

being the last to be closed by BR (1985), though it was hardly a return to Beeching: more stations opened than closed during the 1980s, particularly where PTE support was forthcoming. In all, 160 were to live again, while the West Yorkshire, Greater Manchester and Tyne & Wear PTEs also contributed to the cost of 'Pacer' units for use by Provincial around Leeds, Bradford, Manchester, Newcastle and Teesside.

Seen by some as the 'Cinderella' sector, Provincial tended to inherit everyone else's 'cast-offs', particularly on the Cardiff–Portsmouth and Manchester Victoria–Leeds routes, where older rolling stock reigned supreme. This process – 'cascading' – was an economical way to redeploy carriages and locomotives when funds for new equipment were in short supply. Loved by enthusiasts, who regularly knocked off numbers and racked up miles across the country, it hardly created a 'go ahead' image, despite the application of new liveries – though cases of new liveries boosting receipts were not unknown, as Chris Green would soon discover.

As General Manager of the Scottish Region, Green (who joined BR as a management trainee in 1965) was instrumental in creating a new 'ScotRail' brand for services north of the border. Under his tenure, steam returned to Fort William in a bid to increase tourist traffic, while a pool of Class 37s were fitted with electric train heating to facilitate the use of more modern carriages on Far North and West Highland services.

The Highlands (and Provincial) were also to benefit from Radio Electronic Token Block (RETB), a communication system which linked cab to signal cabin and dispensed with the need for line-side equipment such as cables, telegraph poles – and the signals themselves. Trialled between Dingwall and Kyle of Lochalsh in 1984, it was later installed on the Wick/Thurso,

Fort William, Mallaig and Oban lines, allowing several staffed signal boxes to be closed. By the end of 1988, drivers on the East Suffolk and the Cambrian were also requesting permission to proceed by radio.

This quest for cost-effective efficiency was evident too on London & South East (LSE). Here, Sector Director David Kirby had managed to cut his PSO requirement by just over a third, reacting to a reduction in demand by withdrawing redundant stock and running fewer, shorter, trains. With much of LSE's revenue coming from commuters, his only hope for a large increase in revenue was a new non-stop service linking London Victoria with Gatwick, devised to tap into a rise in air travel. The trains made good use of older air-conditioned 'Mark II' carriages and Class 73 electro-diesels, while 'push-pull' working with a powered 'motor luggage van' afforded a quick turnaround and an intense 15-minute timetable. Launched in May 1984, the 'Gatwick Express' was so successful that a new line to Stansted Airport was authorised in 1986, and plans to link with Manchester and Heathrow airports were well under way by 1990.

Kirby had also enhanced LSE's image by introducing a brown and orange ('Jaffa cake') Sector livery, but it was the arrival of Green in January 1986 that would bring more radical change. Under Green, London & South East was given a catchier title – Network SouthEast (NSE) – and a striking red, white and blue colour scheme. It was also expanded to

BREL was rationalised, reorganised and sold in 1989. Closure of the former Great Western Railway works at Swindon had come in 1986. The town would later re-invent itself, but many trained coppersmiths and electricians would never ply their trade again.

bring together all commuter routes into the capital, regardless of Region. As a result, NSE stretched for 2,350 route miles across the Southern, along with parts of the Western, London Midland, and Eastern. To advertise – and galvanise – the new business, Green modernised his 930 stations 'ScotRail style', which meant branding anything and everything and saw red fencing, litter bins, lamp-posts and clocks spring up on platforms from Weymouth to Banbury, Bedwyn, Brighton, King's Lynn, Clacton and Shoeburyness. Trialled on the 'Chiltern' line out of London Marylebone, it soon won a following, got the Sector noticed and helped boost receipts. Green also started an initiative which allowed passengers to travel anywhere on NSE for just £3.00; on the first of these 'Network Days' – 21 June 1986 – 200,000 people took up the offer, most (as Green would later recall) seemingly bent on getting to the Isle of Wight!

InterCity timetable from 1986–7. Note that the Sector dispensed with the hyphen that graced the original brand.

As the inheritor of the APT, InterCity had a slightly different problem. After the disastrous attempt to run a public service, the train had become something of a national joke. This was not only disheartening, it was bad for business. In a bid to move the project forward, the Board brought in a team of consultants, who concluded that the technology was generally sound, but that the management team lacked leadership and vision (although this charge could also have been levelled at the government). BR duly appointed a dedicated project manager and soon 'got a grip' – so much so that by 1983, the trains were beginning to work well and by December 1984 had set a new record of 3 hours 52 minutes for the Euston to Glasgow run.

Sadly, it was a victory too late, for the fact was that even these timings were no longer enough to tempt Anglo-Scottish travellers away from air travel. However, InterCity knew that by raising the maximum speed of certain key expresses from 100mph to 110mph, and by adding more station stops, it could capture the key markets of Manchester, the West Midlands and Lancashire, which were all within the critical three-hour threshold from London wherein the train could match the plane.

When the APT programme was abandoned in 1986, InterCity also switched emphasis to the quality of service: on-board catering improved, 'Second Class' became 'Standard Class' and named trains were reborn, meaning that passengers could catch the 'Cornish Riviera' to Cornwall or the 'Master Cutler' to Sheffield just as in the glory days of steam. Thankfully, Reid's success in forging good relations with the Conservative government would soon bring electrification to Cambridge, Norwich and Weymouth – though it was the East Coast Main Line that needed it most: since the demise of the 'Deltics' in 1982, the route had been in the hands of eight-car HSTs; when passenger numbers rose later in the decade, many people found themselves forced to stand in the carriage aisles and vestibules, setting off the internal sliding doors to no-one's advantage.

Government approval for electrifying this premier line finally came in July 1984 and brought the prospect of more powerful locomotives, which could haul longer trains. Various options were considered, but the front-runner was a 5,850-hp, 125-mph machine, which would work with 'Mark III' coaches and a driving trailer, similar to the Glasgow–Edinburgh push-pull services. A prototype – 89001 – was built jointly by

Reid's investment success was not limited to electrification: the government also approved the purchase of new rolling stock for NSE and Provincial. The latter's Sprinter (Class 150), Super Sprinter (155-6) and Express (158) units were to transform the speed and quality of many journeys. Here, 156439 calls at Dumfries.

Brush Traction and BREL. By the time it appeared in 1986, however, InterCity director John Prideaux – mindful that BR's reputation rested largely on InterCity's performance – had decided that 140 mph was needed. This led to the 6,000-hp GEC-built Class 91, with which came new 'Mark IV' carriages and a new name: the 'InterCity 225'. This – while a nod to the fact that 140 mph is 225 km/h – also helped create distance from the APT and affinity with the more successful HST.

Electric services began between King's Cross and Peterborough on 3 March 1989, trains to Leeds following eleven days later. Unfortunately, and despite Prideaux's wish, the Class 91s were never allowed to exceed 125 mph, because of the government's reluctance to approve the necessary upgrade of the signalling system. Cost cutting also meant that the supporting masts had to be placed further apart than the engineer would have liked, which often resulted in the wires drooping or blowing down in high winds. As Reid would later comment: 'You may have to do what you suspect will be wrong in the long term for very sound reasons in the short term.'

Like nationalisation, modernisation and rationalisation before it, sectorisation brought some of the biggest post-war changes to the railway. True, the new liveries often helped hide an ageing fleet, but Reid's efforts to win investment cash, coupled with continuing subsidiary sell-offs, land sales, staff reductions and an increasing use of computers for ticketing and delay monitoring, saw BR's finances start to shape up – so much so that

The experimental 89001 moves off Crewe depot with a test train in August 1987.

in 1989 InterCity became the first nationalised rail network in the world to run at a profit. NSE and Provincial also made inroads into their deficits, while Railfreight's block train business proved it had weathered the national coal miners' dispute of 1984–5 by producing a useful surplus.

For Parcels, though, the outlook was darker, owing to News International's contract-breaking withdrawal from rail (which led to the end of all newspaper traffic by July 1988), and the Royal Mail's decision to transfer more of its operation to other modes. It was the same for Speedlink, whose salesmen were winning business ever further from the core network, meaning that the cost of tripping wagons from main yard to customer began to outstrip income. Its resemblance to the wagonload operation it was meant to replace made the 1988 amalgamation with Freightliner inevitable. Yet for this new company – Railfreight Distribution – hope came in the form of new business via the Channel Tunnel – a Victorian idea supported by Marsh, cancelled by Whitehall, rekindled by Parker, and finally ratified by the British and French governments in 1986.

As the decade drew to a close, work would be well under way on this impressive project, and what with the sympathetic redevelopment of London Liverpool Street, East Coast electrification, increasing productivity, more stations, rising passenger numbers and falling subsidies, it seemed that sectorisation *was* working, that a golden age for BR really *was* dawning. Then came Clapham.

91011 passes Brookmans Park sporting InterCity's final livery. Originally known as 'Electra', the '91s' worked in push-pull mode with nine plug-door 'Mark IV' carriages and a driving van trailer (DVT). The profiled sides were intended to facilitate possible tilt mechanism fitment (sadly never adopted).

By the late 1980s, resignalling schemes had been commissioned or completed at Brighton, Newcastle, York, Leeds, Leicester and Waterloo. The last was a particularly big operation, involving the replacement of equipment on the busiest stretch of railway in Britain. On the evening of 27 November 1988, an overtired, under-trained technician left a live wire dangling in a relay room at Clapham Junction 'A', a huge signal box on a gantry that spanned a sea of lines at the station throat. Two weeks later, further work jolted the wire, causing it to touch a terminal, make a connection and prevent a signal from returning to danger after the passage of a train.

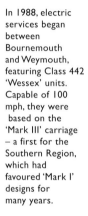

In 1988, electric services began between Bournemouth and Weymouth, featuring Class 442 'Wessex' units. Capable of 100 mph, they were based on the 'Mark III' carriage – a first for the Southern Region, which had favoured 'Mark I' designs for many years.

Just after 8 a.m. on Monday 12 December, a commuter service was enjoying a clear run on its way in from the South Coast. Green light followed green light: the usual story – except that the last one should have been red. As the train rounded the curve, its driver saw another blocking the line ahead. He applied the emergency brake, but it was too late. The collision forced the leading coach to the side, where it struck an empty unit passing in the opposite direction. Thirty-five people were killed and almost five hundred were injured.

Reid won much respect by visiting the crash site quickly and accepting full responsibility on behalf of the Board. Yet within a few months, the questions about standards, staff cuts and chains of command some had raised on the eve

In 1986, the first US-built Class 59 was delivered to Britain for Foster Yeoman, which had become frustrated by locomotive failures and timekeeping on its trains. Though driven by BR drivers, the '59s' were a foretaste of the coming era of privatisation. Here, 59001 leaves Newbury with a train of 'empties' for Merehead Quarry.

of sectorisation would come up again when two fatal 'signal passed at danger' accidents occurred in the space of three days at Purley (4 March 1989) and Bellgrove (6 March 1989). The Clapham inquiry – chaired by Sir Anthony Hidden QC – would lead to changes in signal testing procedures and working hours for staff on 'safety critical' work. As BR reorganised for the 1990s, it also ensured that 'risk management' and 'change management' played a vital part in the decision-making process. Soon, though, the railway would be reorganising for a very different reason: privatisation was on the way.

So too was another recession.

In 1988, BR divided Railfreight into subsectors for coal, construction, metals, petroleum and general traffic. It also ordered 100 3,100hp Class 60 diesels to reinforce its place in the heavy haulage market. In this view, brand-new 60004 *Lochnagar* shows off the 'Trainload Coal' subsector livery.

PLACES TO VISIT

MUSEUMS

Barrow Hill Roundhouse Railway Centre, Campbell Drive, Barrow Hill, Chesterfield,
Derbyshire S43 2PR. Telephone: 01246 472450. Website: www.barrowhill.org
Britain's only surviving, operational roundhouse engine shed; frequently holds
modern traction events.

Crewe Heritage Centre, Vernon Way, Crewe, Cheshire CW1 2DB. Telephone: 01270
212130. Website: www.creweheritagecentre.co.uk
Includes the APT-P, among other traction exhibits; also offers the chance to
drive a diesel locomotive on its demonstration line.

National Railway Museum, Leeman Road, York YO26 6XJ. Telephone: 01926 621261.
Website: www.nrm.org.uk   Home of HSDT power car 41001.

'Locomotion', the National Railway Museum at Shildon, Shildon, County Durham DL4
1PQ. Telephone: 01388 777999.
Website: www.nrm.org.uk/PlanaVisit/VisitShildon.aspx   Includes the APT-E.

HERITAGE RAILWAYS

A number of Britain's heritage railways feature locomotives, rolling stock
and infrastructure that were used throughout the 1970s and '80s. For more details,
see the Heritage Railway Association website: www.heritagerailways.com
Of particular interest are:

Bo'ness and Kinneil Railway, The Scottish Railway Preservation Society, Bo'ness
Station, Union Street, Bo'ness, West Lothian EH51 9AQ.
Telephone: 01506 822298. Website: www.srps.org.uk/railway
Home to a large collection of diesel power common to Scotland during
the 1970s and '80s.

Great Central Railway, Loughborough, Leicestershire LE11 1RW.
Telephone: 01509 230726. Website: www.gcrailway.co.uk
The only double-track heritage line in Britain.

Llangollen Railway, The Station, Abbey Road, Llangollen, Denbighshire LL20 8SN.
Telephone: 01978 860979. Website: www.llangollen-railway.co.uk
Operates a variety of locomotives, along with several 'first generation' diesel
multiple units.

The Midland Railway, Butterley Station, Ripley, Derbyshire DE5 3QZ.
Telephone: 01773 747674. Website: www.midlandrailwaycentre.co.uk
The Midland Railway Trust's large collection includes many diesel locomotives
and multiple units from the BR era.

Nene Valley Railway, Wansford Station, Stibbington, Peterborough PE8 6LR.
Telephone: 01780 784444. Website: www.nvr.org.uk

Home to some diesel locomotives and has plans to create a 'travelling post office' museum.

North Yorkshire Moors Railway, 12 Park Street, Pickering, North Yorkshire YO18 7AJ. Telephone: 01751 472508. Website: www.nymr.co.uk Offers occasional 'diesel galas'.

Spa Valley Railway, West Station, Royal Tunbridge Wells, Kent TN2 5QY. Telephone: 01892 537715. Website: www.spavalleyrailway.co.uk 5½-mile branch between Eridge and Tunbridge Wells West – the last to be closed by BR.

Swanage Railway, Station House, Railway Station Approach, Swanage, Dorset BH19 1HB. Telephone: 01929 425800. Website: www.swanagerailway.co.uk Offers occasional 'diesel galas'.

Vale of Rheidol Railway, Park Avenue, Aberystwyth, Ceredigion SY23 1PG. Telephone: 01970 625819. Website: www.rheidolrailway.co.uk 11¾-mile narrow-gauge line from Aberystwyth to Devil's Bridge, opened in 1902 and nationalised in 1948. After the end of mainline steam twenty years later, it became BR's only steam operation until its sale in 1989.

West Somerset Railway, The Railway Station, Minehead, Somerset TA24 5BG. Telephone: 01643 704996. Website: www.west-somerset-railway.co.uk 26-mile heritage line through the Quantocks.

FURTHER READING AND VIEWING

This book is intended to be a sketch of British railway history in the 1970s and '80s and is not, therefore, an exhaustive survey. More detailed information may be found in the following volumes:

Bagwell, Philip S. *The Railwaymen: The History of the National Union of Railwaymen – Volume 2: The Beeching Era and After*. HarperCollins, 1982.

Bonavia, Michael R. *British Rail: The First 25 Years*. David & Charles, 1981.

Boocock, Colin. *Spotlight on BR: British Railways 1949–1998 – Success or Disaster?* Atlantic, 1998.

Dobrzynski, Jan. *British Railway Tickets*. Shire, 2011. The story of railway tickets, from the type invented by Thomas Edmondson in 1838 to modern day practice. Also includes information on collecting.

Gourvish, T. R. *British Railways 1948–73: A Business History*. Cambridge University Press, 1986.

Gourvish, T. R. *British Railways 1974–97: A Business History*. Cambridge University Press, 1986.

Gregory, Anthony. *Life on the Leicester Line: The Progress of a Train Driver*. P. Way Publishing, 2002. Driver Gregory tells the story of how it was at the front line during a period of change; includes observations on the 1982 ASLEF/NUR strikes and the 1984/5 miners' strike.

Griffiths, Robert. *Driven by Ideals: A History of ASLEF*. ASLEF, 2005. Includes the 1982 strike from ASLEF's point of view.

Gwynne, Bob. *Railway Preservation in Britain*. Shire, 2011. Includes notes on steam's return to the main line in 1971.

Haresnape, Brian. *British Rail 1948–1978: A Journey by Design*. Ian Allan, 1979. Covers the design development of locomotives, rolling stock, coach interiors, uniforms, ferries, stations, typefaces and so on.

Henshaw, David. *The Great Railway Conspiracy: The Rise and Fall of Britain's Railways Since the 1950s*. Leading Edge, 1991. An in-depth study of railway closures and political meddling.

Johnson, John, and Long, Robert A. *British Railway Engineering 1948–80*. Mechanical Engineering Publications Ltd, 1981. The engineering story, told by engineers, and edited by former BR Chief Mechanical Engineer R. C. Bond.

Leith, Prue. *Relish: My Life on a Plate*. Quercus, 2012. Restaurateur and caterer Leith became the first woman to sit on the British Railways Board, being invited by Parker to 'uncurl the sandwiches' in 1980. She totally transformed Travellers Fare, improving its products and presiding over the creation of the successful Casey Jones, Upper Crust and Quicksnack brands.

Marsh, Richard. *Off the Rails: An Autobiography*. Weidenfeld & Nicolson, 1978. The first BR Chairman to write his own story, Marsh (1971–6) details his early life and his time in Parliament before discussing the joys and frustrations of running British Rail.

Morse, Greg. *British Railways in the 1950s and '60s*. Shire, 2012. The 'prequel' to this book.

Parker, Peter. *For Starters: The Business of Life*. Jonathan Cape, 1989. Parker's autobiography includes insights into his refusal to take the BR Chair in the 1960s, his struggles to secure investment, his take on the ASLEF strike of 1982 and the Serpell Report of 1983.

Poole, Stephen. *Behind the Crumbling Edge: A View of the Nationalised Railway*. Book Guild, 2002. Stories of camaraderie, frustration and survival during a period of social, industrial, financial and political change. Includes a foreword by Parker.

Williams, Hugh. *APT: A Promise Unfulfilled*. Ian Allan, 1985. The story of the ill-fated project told by the former APT-E Train Supervisor.

Wojtczak, Helena. *Railwaywomen: Exploitation, Betrayal and Triumph in the Workplace*. Hastings Press, 2003. A book of pioneers, of whom Wojtczak was one, becoming the first female guard to be employed by British Rail in 1979.

Wolmar, Christian. *Fire and Steam: A New History of the Railways in Britain*. Atlantic Books, 2007.

Class 71 electric 71007 at London Victoria in April 1974 with the stock from the 'Night Ferry'. Note the third rail, from which 750 DC power is collected by 'shoes' on the locomotive or unit (visible here).

Plenty of photographic albums featuring BR in the 1970s and '80s are also available, while most of the source documents referred to in this book – including the Serpell Report and the inquiry into the Clapham Junction accident – may be downloaded free of charge from the Railways Archive website: www.railwaysarchive.co.uk

The British Film Institute has released a number of British Transport Films' finest documentaries on DVD. Other films available on DVD include:

Get Carter (1971). Revenge film with Michael Caine, which begins with his character taking a first-class trip from King's Cross to Newcastle. The scenes feature many elements gone from today's railway, like corridor trains, smoking in the compartment and white-waistcoated waiters serving four-course meals in the restaurant car. The film was shot long before the East Coast Main Line was electrified, at a time when it was still controlled by a forest of semaphore signals and when the station name boards at Newcastle still wore the tangerine background of BR's North Eastern Region.

Night Ferry (1977). Children's Film Foundation crime drama with Bernard Cribbins. Scenes include traditional hump shunting, typical mid-1970s Southern Region commuter trains, and the celebrated London Victoria–Paris 'Night Ferry', a service which would run for the last time in October 1980.

Confessions of a Train Spotter (1980). This episode in the BBC Television series *Great Railway Journeys of the World* sees Michael Palin take a trip from Euston to Kyle of Lochalsh, stopping overnight at BR's North British Hotel, Edinburgh, on the way. Also includes interviews with a BR stewardess, a signalwoman from the Eastern Region, an HST driver, a Railman from the Kyle line and various passengers.

Give My Regards to Broad Street (1984). Paul McCartney's musical extravaganza ends with a night-time scene at London's Broad Street station, which closed in 1986.

Clockwise (1986). Comedy of errors starring John Cleese, featuring a contemporary departure scene at Hull Paragon station.

INDEX